This book
belongs to:

....

....

Do You Have A Secret?

Text: *Jennifer Moore-Mallinos*

Illustrations: *Marta Fàbrega*

BARRON'S

Do you have a secret?
Is it a good secret or a bad secret?

Did you know that good secrets are things that can make you and somebody else very happy?
Can you think of a good secret?

4-5

If you kept a secret about a special birthday present you made for your best friend or your Mom or Dad, would this be a good secret or a bad secret?

You're right! This kind of good secret is okay to keep, because it will always bring a smile to that special someone's face when they see their present.

Can you think of a good secret that
is fun to keep?
Keeping a secret about your brother
or sister's surprise party can be so much fun!

Just imagine the look on their faces when you yell "'SURPRISE!"

What about a special handshake you share
with your best friend? Would that be a secret
that is okay to keep?
I think so, too! Fancy handshakes are fun
secrets to have.

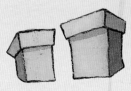

Have you ever played hide-and-seek and helped your best friend find a hiding place?

Helping your friend find a safe hiding place so they won't get caught is a secret that is fun to keep.

Do you want to know my secret? Really?
At nighttime, I like to sleep with my teddy bear,
named Fuzzy. When I'm scared, Fuzzy makes me
feel warm and cozy.
What about you? Do you have a good secret?

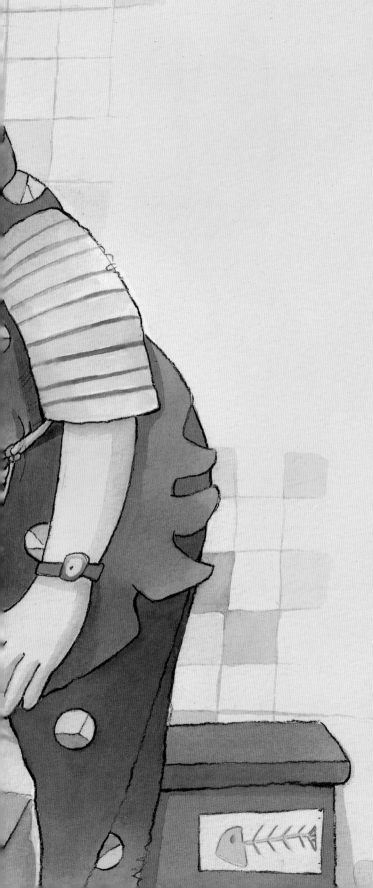

But what is a bad secret?
Did you know that bad secrets
are things that don't make you
feel happy on the inside?
Bad secrets can sometimes
worry you a lot.
The only way to make you feel
better and happy again is to
tell a grown-up your secret.

If you kept a secret about somebody who hurt you, because they hit or kicked or even punched you, would this be a good secret or a bad secret? You're right! It would be a bad secret because it is not okay for somebody to hurt you.

What would you do if you saw the bigger kids at your school take a smaller kid's lunch money? Would it be okay to keep this a secret? You're right! It's not okay!

Just because the big kids are older and taller, it doesn't make it okay for them to take something that does not belong to them.

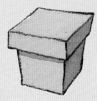 Can you think of another kind of bad secret?
Would you keep it a secret if somebody touched
you in a way that made you feel uncomfortable
and all yucky inside? This kind
of secret is a bad secret and
that means you need to get
the help of a grown-up so
you can feel better.

Do you think it is okay to keep a bad secret if someone asked you to? Of course not! It is not okay for somebody who has done something that they are not supposed to do, to tell you to keep it a secret. It is a bad secret, and you need to tell a grown-up.

And who can this grown-up be? This person should be someone you trust, like your Mom or your Dad, or your aunt or your uncle, or even your teacher at school. Telling a bad secret is a very good thing to do!

Don't forget, secrets can be fun to keep, especially if they are things that will make you and somebody else very happy. These kinds of secrets are good and they are okay to keep. But keeping a secret about something that hurt you on the outside, or made you feel sad or scared on the inside, is not a good idea. The best thing to do if you have a bad secret is to always tell a grown-up. Telling a grown-up your secret can sometimes feel like a hard thing to do. So, try to be brave and remember, that telling your secret is not only the right thing to do, but it will help to make you feel better.

Do you have a secret?

Note
to parents

Throughout my experience as a child welfare social worker, I have developed a good understanding of the various difficulties many children face in today's society. Given our increased awareness that child abuse (physical, sexual, emotional, and neglectful) occurs so readily, we, as parents, and professionals, need to take an active role in our attempts to protect our children.

Providing our children with the opportunity to gain a solid knowledge base, in respect to their safety, is not only our responsibility, but it is the right thing to do. When children are encouraged to communicate, they will, in turn, develop the appropriate skills necessary for them to be active participants in maintaining their own safety.

The purpose of "Do You Have A Secret?" is to stimulate dialogue and instill knowledge. Children, parents, and professionals will learn to distinguish between "good secrets" and those secrets that are necessary to disclose.

A child's ability to distinguish such information will have a positive impact on his/her ability to react appropriately. When a child feels empowered through knowledge, he/she will ultimately be more in control of their own safety.

Children are always encouraged to ask and answer the questions posed throughout the book. Dialogue is created as a means to initiate communication, and to inspire learning.

Children spend much of their time away from the security of their own homes, and as a result, we are not always able to be with them to ensure their safety. What we can do however, is introduce knowledge and encourage communication, so our children feel comfortable enough to disclose their secrets, whether they are good or bad.

If your child discloses a bad secret, it is recommended that you seek the assistance of a professional such as law enforcement, and/or child protection services. If you are not sure where to turn, ask your family physician to recommend the best place to find the appropriate support and assistance you need.

Children are motivated to learn when they are having fun. Therefore, the most effective way to share these concepts is simply that...have fun!

As you read this book to your child, allow your enthusiasm and interest in the book's message to be heard. By engaging your child's interest, and allowing him or her to participate in the fun, the book's message will be conveyed.

First edition for the United States and Canada published in 2005
by Barron's Educational Series, Inc.
Original title of the book in Spanish: ¿ *Tienes un Secreto?*
© Copyright 2005 by Gemser Publications S.L.
C/Castell, 38; Teià (08329) Barcelona, Spain (World Rights)
Author: Jennifer Moore-Mallinos
Illustrator: Marta Fàbrega

All inquiries should be addressed to:
Barron's Educational Series, Inc.
250 Wireless Boulevard
Hauppauge, New York 11788
http://www.barronseduc.com

ISBN:978-0-7641-3170-7
Library of Congress Control Number: 2004112882

Printed in China
Manufactured by: L.Rex Printing Company Limited, Dongguan, China
Date of Manufacture: March 2016
19 18 17 16 15 14 13 12 11 10